CONTENTS

6   **Sinnoh Sum-up**

8   **Enter Ash And Pikachu!**

10   **Brock Stop!**

12   **Definitely Dawn!**

14   **Team Rocket Time**

16   **Land Of Legends**

17   **Dialga and Palkia 3D Poster**

18   **Ways Through The Waves**

19   **Choose Your Cherrim!**

20   **All Of A Dozen!**

22   **Unlocking The Red Chain Of Events! Story**

30   **Team Rocket Challenges YOU!**

32   **Bug-type Colour Jumble**

33   **Team Galactic Pokémon 3D Poster**

34   **Rule It Out!**

35   **Habitat Match**

36   **New Moves**

37   **Make Your Own Compass**

38   **Poké Purple!**

39   **Ash And Friends 3D Poster**

40   **The Needs Of The Three! Story**

48   **Golbat Attack!**

49   **Pokémon Field Report**

50   **Not My Type!**

52   **Umbreon and Electivire 3D Poster**

53   **Pokémon Power**

54   **Follow The Ladders!**

56   **Mirror Mirror**

57   **Double Bluff!**

58   **The Battle Finale of Legend! Story**

66   **The Lake Trio 3D Poster**

68   **Answers**

CW01083696

Pedigree®

Published 2011.
Pedigree Books Ltd, Beech Hill House,
Walnut Gardens, Exeter, Devon EX4 4DH
books@pedigreegroup.co.uk
www.pedigreebooks.com

£6.99

SINNOH SUM-UP

Are you ready to step into Sinnoh and share some awesome 3D adventures with Ash and his pals? This knockout activity book is the one for you! This brand new edition sees the heroes nearing the end of their journey in this vast and beautiful region – anyone would agree that it's been quite a ride!

Sinnoh is a diverse and rugged land, home to a dazzling array of Pokémon species. The craggy peak Mt. Coronet marks the centre of the region, dividing it into two majestic halves. On either side of the mountains, bustling cities nestle between thick forest, sparkling lakes and fertile valleys.

Sinnoh also boasts miles and miles of undulating coastline, with untold Pokémon leaping and diving in the oceans all around.

Since Ash and Brock met Dawn at Twinleaf Town, the trio have trekked up and down Sinnoh, visiting many of its finest Gyms. Each skilful Gym Leader has taught the crew a new wisdom about the art of training and battling Pokémon. Ash will never forget taking on Roark at the Oreburgh Gym or travelling to Snowpoint City to challenge Candice!

Who knows where Ash's quest will take him next? Sinnoh has presented the Trainer with a host of challenges, shocks and surprises, but he's still sure the best is yet to come!

MAP HAPPY

How much do you really know about Sinnoh's cities and landmarks? Take this quick tick test and discover if you're an expert explorer or a Sinnoh stranger!

1. Professor Rowan's Pokémon lab is located in Sandgem Town.

True ☐   False ☐

2. Eterna is the name of a large sea.

True ☐   False ☐

3. The temple in Snowpoint City is said to contain a Legendary Pokémon.

True ☐   False ☐

4. The Pastoria Great Marsh is now very dry and arid.

True ☐   False ☐

5. Canalave City has a chilly, mountain location.

True ☐   False ☐

6. The Poketch corporation is based in Jubilife City.

True ☐   False ☐

7. The region has no known islands located off its coastline.

True ☐   False ☐

8. Sinnoh has five Pokémon Gyms.

True ☐   False ☐

ENTER ASH AND PIKACHU

These pages are crammed with facts and stats about Ash, his pals and his enemies too, but you'll need to do some puzzling before you can enjoy them fully. What are you waiting for? **GRAB SOME PENS AND GET CRACKING!**

ASH PROFILE

FILL IN THE BLANKS TO BRING THIS PROFILE PANEL TO LIFE...

Ash Ketchum is a determined young _ _ _ _ _ _ _ _ who's come a long way since he first left his home in _ _ _ _ _ _ _ _ Town! Through determination, skill and hard work he's managed to earn himself a batch of _ _ _ _ _ _ _ _ _ that would make any Pokémon Trainer proud! Some, like Ash's rival, _ _ _ _ _, might say that the youngster is hasty and hot-headed, but his refusal to give up has awarded him the edge in many _ _ _ _ _ _ _ _ battles!

PIKACHU

Pikachu is an unusual first companion for any young Trainer, but Ash doesn't regret choosing him for a second. Pikachu is courageous and loyal to its friend, always ready to leap off Ash's shoulder and take action if danger looms near.

TYPE: ....
.....................: STATIC
HEIGHT: 0.4M
WEIGHT: 6.0KG

THIS POKÉMON DWELLS IN FORESTS AND WOODLANDS, LIVING IN GROUPS. IT USES ITS CHEEK POUCHES TO STORE .... PIKACHU IS EVOLVED FROM ....

PIKACHU

Can you complete the Pikachu facts in this Pokédex screen?

So you've sussed out Pikachu, but what about the rest? Unjumble the anagrams to reveal all the names of Ash's loyal Pokémon crew!

2. ELTDRG

3. ZILUEB

4. LIGEB

5. RDNMOFEN

1. TDTPARARS

BROCK

STOP!

Help Brock make a splash by colouring in this cool picture of him with his loyal Pokémon – Happiny, Sudowoodo and Croagunk. Find the mini-poster from the sticker sheet, fix it in place, then get to work with your favourite felt-tips!

BROCK

Ash's pal and trusty travel companion is a one-stop advice shop. Brock has a passion for Pokémon that's second to none, teamed with a jaw-dropping species knowledge – there's no doubt that that he'll make an amazing breeder one day! Brock used to be the Gym Leader in Pewter City, stepping in to hold the fort and care for his brothers and sisters while his father Flint was away. Now he's happy to roam Sinnoh with his friends, meeting new species and learning how to rear Pokémon.

TOP
BROCK FACTS!

Brock can cook up a scrummy feast anytime, anywhere!

The breeder has a cringe-making habit of falling in love with every new lady he meets!

Brock's first ever Pokémon was an Onix.

Write your favourite Brock fact in here.

DEFINITELY DAWN

Look at the amazing bunch of Pokémon that have become loyal to Dawn! Use your knowledge to write the correct name next to each of the Coordinator's friends.

I.

DAWN

Dawn couldn't be happier exploring Sinnoh with her two best friends, Ash and Brock! The enthusiastic follower of fashion loves taking on challenges and building her Pokémon expertise. Dawn has a simple goal – to become a renowned Coordinator, just like her mother Johanna before her. Instead of signing up for the Sinnoh League, she enters Pokémon Contests. She's won and lost some, but her collection of ribbons is growing all the time! Even when times are tough, Dawn puts on a brave face and gives her all. She'd rather look to the future than waste time worrying!

2.

3.

4.

PSST! DAWN HAS TEAMED UP WITH A NEW POKÉMON – DO YOU KNOW WHO IT IS? TAKE A GUESS HERE, THEN TURN TO PAGE 36 TO FIND OUT MORE!

TEAM ROCKET

This terrible team of criminals can usually be found following Ash on all of his adventures! Jessie, James and Meowth are on a mission to swipe Pokémon whenever and wherever they get the chance. They've had their eyes firmly fixed on Ash's Pikachu for some time, but can never quite outwit or out-battle the Trainer and his feisty Electric-type. Meowth talks the talk and plans the plans, while Jessie and James rustle up all kinds of cunning disguises to snare their prey. They've tried every dirty trick in the book, but Team Rocket nearly always end up blasting off!

60
SECOND CHALLENGE

Ready to go head-to-head with Jessie, James and Meowth? Find a stopwatch, then see if you can crack this quick quiz in less than one minute!

1. What makes Team Rocket's Meowth a particularly unusual Pokémon?

....

2. What sort of family does James come from?

....

3. What is the name of Team Rocket's elusive boss?

....

4. What mode of transport do the trio usually use?

....

5. How does Team Rocket describe Ash and his friends?

....

Poké Pals

There are ten Pokémon shown here, but only five of them are loyal to Jessie, James and Meowth. Place a cross next to the ones that travel with Team Rocket.

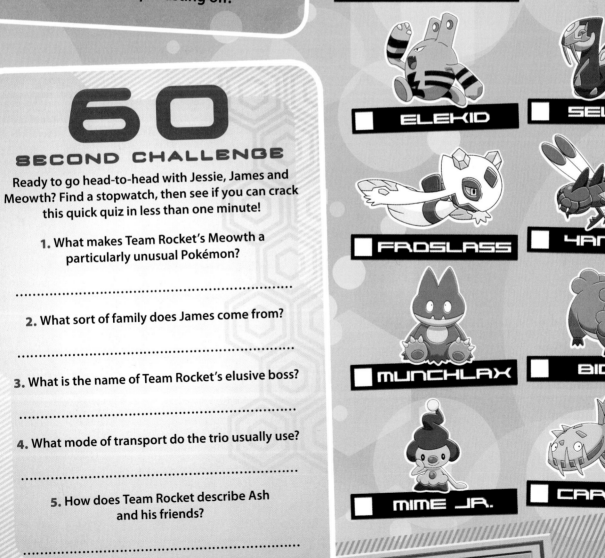

- ☐ WOBBUFFET
- ☐ GEODUDE
- ☐ ELEKID
- ☐ SEVIPER
- ☐ FROSLASS
- ☐ YANMEGA
- ☐ MUNCHLAX
- ☐ BIDOOF
- ☐ MIME JR.
- ☐ CARNIVINE

LAND OF LEGENDS

Dialga and Palkia are giants of Sinnoh mythology. It is said that the Legendary Pokémon have such immense power, they can control time and space itself. There are so many stories about this epic pair, Ash is struggling to sort out fact from fiction!

Can you help him out? Work down this list, ticking the statements that are true.

1. Dialga and Palkia live in other dimensions.
   Fact ☐   Fiction ☐

2. Palkia has the Pressure Ability.
   Fact ☐   Fiction ☐

3. Dialga is a Poison-type Pokémon.
   Fact ☐   Fiction ☐

4. Since ancient times, both Pokémon have featured in Sinnoh legends.
   Fact ☐   Fiction ☐

5. Palkia has the ability to distort matter.
   Fact ☐   Fiction ☐

6. Statues of them are sometimes found near ancient ruins.
   Fact ☐   Fiction ☐

7. Dialga has a distinctive crest and an orange tail plume.
   Fact ☐   Fiction ☐

8. Dialga has no Evolutions.
   Fact ☐   Fiction ☐

9. Neither Dialga nor Palkia are over 2 metres tall.
   Fact ☐   Fiction ☐

10. Palkia is a Water- and Dragon-type Pokémon.
    Fact ☐   Fiction ☐

PALKIA

Type: WATER-DRAGON
Ability: Pressure
Height: 4.2m
Weight: 336.0kg

DIALGA

Type: STEEL-DRAGON
Ability: Pressure
Height: 5.4m
Weight: 683.0kg

DIALGA AND PALKIA

LEGENDARY POKÉMON

RULERS OF TIME AND SPACE

WAYS THROUGH
THE WAVES

Brock has heard a report of a Phione in trouble, out in the waters off the Sinnoh coast! Help the breeder pull off a high-speed rescue, by taking him on the quickest route across the ocean.

Colour in the Pokémon you spot along the way – your route should pass at least four species!

START

CHOOSE YOUR CHERRIM!

The sun has come out, filling this page with blooming Cherrim! Somewhere amongst this group of Grass-types there is an identical pair of Pokémon. Use your honed powers of observation to study the Cherrim at the top, then circle its exact match below.

ALL OF A DOZEN!

Look at this awesome collection of Pokémon! There are 12 species gathered on this page, each with its own fascinating Abilities, markings and characteristics. Show off your Trainer skills by writing the correct name next to each picture. Can you complete the dozen?

_____

IGUASMSIM

_____

LIARDES

_____

MELAWDG

_____

RDIDLDNF

_____

MRDDT

_____

RDADNIP

_____

BDECEM

_____

CDUALIR

_____

PEMDNEDL

_____

HDR4ERPIR

_____

WUTIRTG

_____

SDNEUR

When you've cracked the name game, it's time to find each Pokémon on the word grid. The names could be running in any direction – forwards, backwards, diagonally and vertically. Happy hunting!

D	J	K	W	O	E	M	A	L	G	Q	T
F	E	M	P	O	L	E	O	N	X	T	U
H	S	P	N	I	D	W	O	F	G	R	R
C	A	T	B	R	F	R	S	R	T	S	T
O	A	Y	I	A	K	C	N	C	K	U	W
M	I	B	Y	C	R	O	O	E	Y	I	I
B	L	G	T	U	O	B	V	D	G	G	G
E	E	F	G	L	T	W	E	G	D	A	K
E	S	X	F	P	O	T	R	N	S	M	Y
A	O	I	W	L	M	G	B	M	Z	S	I
S	R	H	Y	P	E	R	I	O	R	I	O
D	R	A	P	I	O	N	U	U	S	M	Q

UNLOCKING THE...
RED CHAIN
OF EVENTS!

Continuing toward Ash's next Gym battle in Sunyshore City, our heroes have opted in favour of a long-awaited rest in Floaroma Town. Pikachu and Piplup lead the way through through a stunning meadow of wild flowers…

Ash, Brock and Dawn were chatting excitedly about Pokémon Contests, when they came across a small figure slumped in the blooms ahead. It was a Meowth.

"It looks bad," said Dawn, bending over the unconscious and battered Pokémon.

Piplup and Pikachu shook it gently. Suddenly the injured Meowth opened its eyes and sprang upright.

"Yipes! It's the Twoips!" it spluttered.

"It's Team Rocket's Meowth!" Ash exclaimed.

The Trainer was right – but where were Jessie and James?

Before Meowth could explain how he came to be parted from his crew, he collapsed again. This time, Brock's breeder expertise was on-hand to revive him.

"What happened to you anyway?" Ash asked, while Brock gently dressed Meowth's wounds.

"It was those fashion freaks," Meowth snarled. "See, we were tailin' you Twoips, doin' that ting that we do so well…"

Ash, Brock, Dawn, Pikachu and Piplup listened intently as Meowth described exactly how he'd come to be lying unconscious and alone in a flower-filled meadow.

According to Meowth, Team Rocket had been foraging for food in the forest when they spotted a helicopter flying overhead.

Jessie instantly recognised the chopper as belonging to their sworn rivals, Team Galactic! Team Galactic were a villainous group of criminals, with a reputation for being ruthless.

Jessie, James and Meowth discovered that the helicopter had taken off from an industrial plant, which lay hidden amongst the trees. Could it be that they'd finally discovered Team Galactic's base?

While Meowth told his story, Brock consulted his Pokédex.

"Is this what you saw?" he interrupted, showing Meowth a picture on the screen.

Meowth nodded.

"That's the Fuego Ironworks," said Brock. "It's been abandoned for quite some time."

Meowth continued. Finding a way in to the hidden compound, he, Jessie and James had snuck onto a rooftop above the central courtyard.

Team Rocket had peered down to see Team Galactic's Commander Jupiter, squaring up to the International Police officer known as Looker. The trio had decided to do the right thing for once and step in – with the police on their side they figured they were more likely to defeat Team Galactic anyway.

True to Team Rocket form, all did not go as planned. Jessie, James and Meowth managed to stop Jupiter's Skuntank from attacking Looker, but as a result Jupiter turned her attention on them instead! Jessie and James were captured, whilst Meowth was sent spinning into the air, landing in a sorry heap in the meadow.

"Looker really helped us out and now it's our turn to help him!" Brock added.

Wiping a tear from his eye, Meowth gratefully agreed to lead the friends back to the Ironworks.

Back at Fuego, Jessie, James and Looker were locked in a cell guarded by Jupiter's Skuntank. Jessie attempted to break out, but soon found to her cost that an electric current ran through the bars. Looker apologised for having got the purple pair involved.

Once his tale was finished, Meowth rose and nodded at the group.

"Thanks for da save, Twoip," he said to Brock.

"Where are you going?" Dawn asked.

"Jessie and James are waitin' for me back there," Meowth replied, pointing towards the Ironworks.

Surprised by his courage, Ash, Brock and Dawn decided to accompany the feisty Pokémon. There was another reason for lending a hand – the gang had been friends with Looker ever since they had met on a train to Lake Acuity. If the officer was in trouble, they wanted to help.

When he heard the news, Meowth looked horrified.

"I appreciate you patchin' me up!" he railed. "But you and I are enemies, dig it? I can't take charity from you."

"Think of it like this…" smiled Dawn. "We're helpin' Looker for us!"

"We involved ourselves," argued James. "Our disdain for Team Galactic brought us here! Since we did manage to barge into their base, all that remains is to defeat their boss."

"Their boss isn't here," sighed Looker, explaining that Team Galactic had been using the plant as a secret factory.

"They're using it to make something…"

Suddenly a guard ran in to inform her that a flying object had been spotted within the perimeter of the Ironworks. Jupiter headed upstairs to check out the intruders.

The flying object turned out to be Team Rocket's air balloon containing Meowth, Brock, Ash, Dawn and their Pokémon.

"Dig it guys," bellowed Meowth. "Up ahead!"

Looker was right. In a secret laboratory in the dark basement of the plant, Jupiter and another Team Galactic Commander, Charon, stood back to admire their handiwork.

"Ah, to look upon the exquisite beauty of the Red Chain…" crowed Jupiter, staring at a circle of glowing red stones rotating in the air above her. "It's quite remarkable that we could recreate it from the Veilstone City meteorite."

"Not recreate it, resurrect it," corrected Charon. "The brilliant genius who should be credited with bringing it back into our world is yours truly."

Jupiter turned away and switched on a screen that linked the pair to the Team Galactic headquarters. They watched as their fellow Commander, Saturn, told their leader, Cyrus, that using a powerful object called the Spear Key they had at last found the gateway to Spear Pillar. The quest had been long and arduous, but to Cyrus it was of incalculable significance. What was his evil organisation up to?

"Our searching is over," Jupiter whispered, "but the real journey begins now."

Before the rescue party could make their descent, a swarm of Golbat surrounded Team Rocket's balloon.

Ash called Gliscor and Staraptor out from their Poké Balls, then urged Pikachu and Pachirisu to mount the two bigger Pokémon. Using Thunderbolt and Discharge, the combined forces sent dozens of Golbat plummeting to the ground.

The balloon landed on the roof, but Jupiter was lying in wait with her Skuntank.

"Use Flamethrower," she ordered.

Fiery jets flared from Skuntank's jaws, but Dawn had Piplup counter with BubbleBeam, buying some precious time.

"You all seem to be so good at popping up out of nowhere," cried Jupiter. "Want to join Team Galactic?"

"That would be so ewwww!" yelled Dawn, wrinkling her nose.

Meowth demanded to see Jessie and James, but Jupiter didn't reply. She was transfixed by Ash, Dawn and Brock.

"Oh Mesprit," she gasped, gazing at Dawn.

"Azelf," she called to Ash.

Finally Jupiter turned to Brock, whispering the word "Uxie."

At that moment, the friends shared a collective vision of the three Pokémon, vanishing as suddenly as it had appeared.

Jupiter explained Mesprit, Azelf and Uxie were the Lake Trio – Legendary Pokémon spirits said to reside in the lakes of Sinnoh. For some inexplicable reason, Jupiter believed that the trio had chosen to connect with Ash, Dawn and Brock.

"Why is it that they chose you!" she shouted.

"We were the ones who were supposed to have synchronized with the Lake Trio."

In her anger, Jupiter sent another flock of Golbat to attack Pikachu and Staraptor. In the ensuing battle, Pikachu retaliated with Thunderbolt, Piplup used BubbleBeam and Meowth struck with Fury Swipes.

Jupiter floundered, before Skuntank's Toxic move surrounded her enemies in stinking fumes.

Once the choking fog had cleared and they could breathe again, Ash and his pals found themselves alone.

"That flake flew da coop," spat an exasperated Meowth.

Jupiter had escaped, so there was nothing else for it. The gang would have to search the industrial plant until they found where Jessie, James and Looker were being held prisoner.

After a long search, the group eventually discovered the cell. Pikachu and Piplup worked together to blast down the door.

"It's so good ta see you mugs!" said Meowth, running to greet Jessie and James.

"I had faith in you," Jessie gushed, hugging the emotional Pokémon.

It was a tender, but short-lived moment. Now they were reunited, Team Rocket didn't plan on hanging around for long.

"Hasta la vista Twerps!" said James.

"It's been sublime," added Jessie.

Meowth ran after his friends, but stopped to shout a hasty thank you to Ash, Brock and Dawn.

"I owe ya one, big time!"

Within seconds, Team Rocket were back in their balloon.

"We know those fashion freaks have a fondness for frolicking in the mountains," yelled Jessie, as they soared skywards. "So it's toward Mount Coronet we will go!"

"So Team Galactic escaped again," frowned Looker. "That means my work here is finished."

The despondent police officer led the way outside, taking his pals past a mysterious basement laboratory.

"What's all this?" wondered Dawn.

"This wasn't part of the Fuego Ironworks," said Looker. "It must be Team Galactic's doing!"

The group ran inside, eyeing the bizarre equipment covering every wall. A single red stone gleamed from the laboratory floor. Looker bent and retrieved it, then called in Officer Jenny to analyse the find.

When Officer Jenny had inspected the gem, she set it in a special transmission chamber.

"We'll use this to device to transmit any data from the object directly to police headquarters," she explained.

But no sooner had transmission begun than the monitors began to crackle and buzz wildly. After a loud bang, the face of an angry detective appeared on the screens.

"The data you transmitted to International Police Headquarters has wiped our entire database out!" he yelled.

Looker grimaced. "And Team Galactic's data?"

"Destroyed as well!" snapped the detective. "Retrieval uncertain."

Team Galactic had set a trap, leaving the object behind on purpose!

"It was a warning to stop further investigation or else," decided Looker. "But I'll never give up. The next time Team Galactic is up to something I'll be there to stop them!"

As Dawn, Ash and Brock left the Ironworks, they discussed the strange exchange with Jupiter and the visions of the Lake Pokémon.

"What does it all mean?" Dawn asked.

"I'm not sure," shrugged Ash, "Since all we did was see them…"

"I can't stop wondering how Team Galactic knew all about it," added Brock.

Far away in their mountain headquarters, Team Galactic's leader was in a celebratory mood – all the elements of his evil plan were coming together just as he'd hoped.

"The creation of a new world begins," smirked Cyrus, surveying a collection of extraordinary objects held on podiums before him. "The Spear Key and Spear Pillar, the Adamant Orb and the Lustrous Orb, the Red Chain… now all that remains are the three Lake Pokémon."

"All preparations for the Galactic Bomb are complete," confirmed Saturn.

Cyrus turned to acknowledge the familiar figure that had just appeared on the viewscreen.

"Sorry to keep you waiting Pokémon Hunter J," he smiled. "Please proceed with the Lake Pokémon capture as planned."

Pokémon Hunter J nodded, then logged out to prepare her ship.

So with Team Galactic's evil intentions becoming clearer, it seems all of Sinnoh is to be shaken to its very core. Can Ash and his friends save the day and just what is their link to the Legendary Lake Pokémon? Turn to page 40 to find out!

TEAM ROCKET CHALLENGES YOU!

Jessie, James and Meowth are seriously deluded – they often think they have much more know-how than they actually do. Use this super-tough quiz to show Team Rocket exactly what you've got! When you've worked through all of the questions, check your answers at the back of the book and stick your score in the winner's frame.

TRAINER TIP:

THESE QUESTIONS ARE DELIBERATELY TRICKY – TAKE TIME TO THINK THEM OVER BEFORE YOU WRITE DOWN YOUR ANSWERS.

1. Which of these is Chansey's next Evolution?

a. Happiny   b. Clefable   c. Blissey

2. How does Buizel stay afloat in the water?

a. It has a flotation sac around its middle.
b. It has a floatation sac that inflates like a collar.
c. It has a floatation sac embedded in its tail.

3. Which of these Pokémon have no known Evolutions?

a. Wurmple   b. Chatot   c. Pikachu

4. What type of Pokémon is a Tangela?

a. Grass
b. Rock
c. Ghost

5. What is the name of this Pokémon?

a. Jolteon
b. Espeon
c. Flareon

6. What is Pachirisu also known as?

a. The EleFerret Pokémon
b. The EleMouse Pokémon
c. The EleSquirrel Pokémon

7. This is a close-up shot of which Pokémon?

a. Azumarill
b. Marill
c. Piplup

8. How does Skuntank attack?

a. It bites with huge fangs
b. It sprays toxic fumes from its tail
c. It breathes fire from its mouth

9. Which of these Pokémon has different forms, depending on where it is found?

a. Shellos
b. Togekiss
c. Kirlia

10. Pick the Poison-type out of this trio.

a. Heracross   b. Dustox   c. Gligar

11. Which one of these Pokémon isn't an Evolution of Chimchar?

a. Infernape   b. Aipom   c. Monferno

12. How long is Lickitung's tongue?

a. Three times its height
b. Twice its height
c. Four times its height

13. Identify this impressive Pokémon.

a. Magmortar
b. Magmar
c. Rapidash

14. What is Spiritomb attached to?

a. A crack in an ancient wall
b. A crack in a keystone
c. A crack in an iron gate

15. Which of these Pokémon has the Pure Power Ability?

a. Murkrow   b. Haunter   c. Meditite

How did you do? Find the sticker that matches your score and put it in.

 0-5 Keep on Training!

6-9 Good Effort!

10-13 Great Performance!

 14-15 Top Marks!

31

BUG-TYPE
COLOUR JUMBLE

This jumbled swarm of Bug-types are tricky to see right now. Find a pencil and carefully copy the contents of each square in the small grid into the matching letter square in the larger one. By the time you've finished you'll have a fab hand-drawn picture to show your pals!

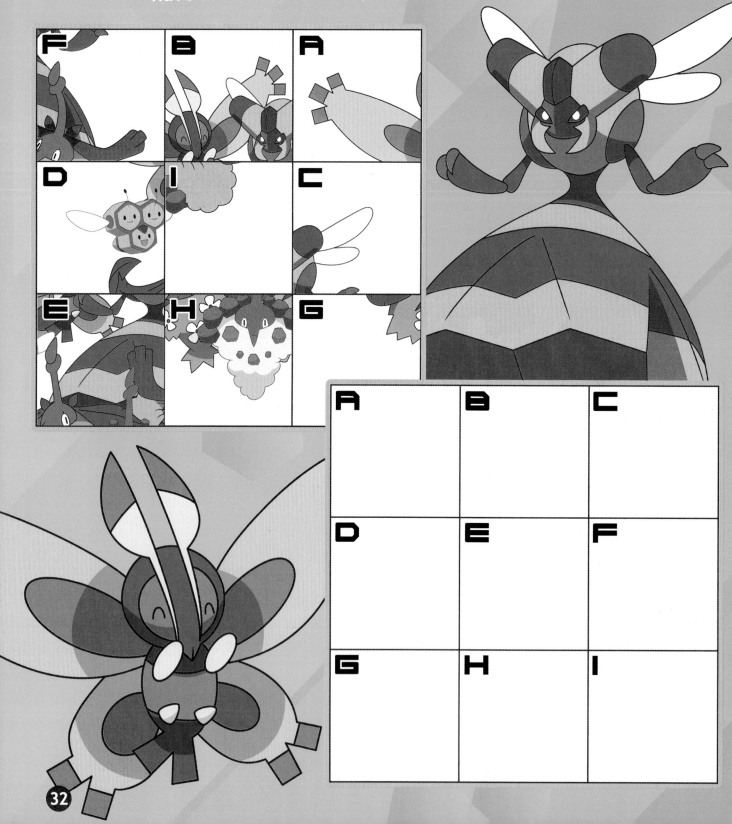

THE POKÉMON OF TEAM GALACTIC

GOLBAT

TOXICROAK

BRONZOR

PURUGLY

SKUNTANK

RULE IT OUT!

An unusual Pokémon has been sighted in Sinnoh! Can you find out which one? Study the nine species below, then use the clues to help you eliminate Pokémon until you get to the right answer.

TYRANITAR	CORPHISH	POLIWAG

SCIZOR	MAGNEMITE	MURKROW
	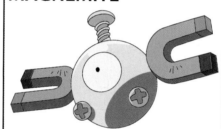	
MISDREAVUS	GRANBULL	TOGEPI

The mystery Pokémon…

- … does not roam on two legs.
- …is underneath a Water-type.
- …is most likely to be seen at night.

Place Sticker here.

Have your deduction skills served you well today? Stick a picture of the correct Pokémon in here, then check your answer on page 68.

HABITAT MATCH

Each species of Pokémon has its unique place in the complex ecosystem of Sinnoh. Find the right colour pictures from the sticker sheet and place them over the silhouettes below. Now draw a line to match each Pokémon up to the environment it likes best.

1. ABOMASNOW

2. CROAGUNK

3. PACHIRISU

4. HIPPOWDON

5. GIBLE

6. BRONZOR

A. Forest and woodland

B. Snowy mountain-tops

C. Ancient tombs

D. Small holes in cave walls

E. Dry, sandy desert

F. Marshes

NEW MOVES

Dawn is thrilled to bits with her latest Pokémon – a fiery Cyndaquil! The new addition to the gang combusts with flames whenever it's time to attack. Dawn is sure that she'll do even better as a Coordinator with young Cyndaquil at her side.

Cyndaquil might be small, but Dawn has learnt from her Piplup that size isn't everything! Take a look at these awesome fighting moves. Three of them are used by Cyndaquil – can you draw a circle round each and every one?

THUNDERBOLT

BLIZZARD

WHIRLPOOL

SWIFT

FLAME WHEEL

THRASH

DIZZY PUNCH

RAZOR LEAF

WING ATTACK

RAZOR WIND

BUBBLEBEAM

SMOKESCREEN

FOUND YOUR THREE?

Now colour in Dawn looking proudly at her new pal!

MAKE YOUR OWN COMPASS

There have been rare occasions where Ash, Dawn and Brock have got lost on their travels – sometimes in the most uninviting places! Sometimes they can use their digital devices to find their bearings but at other times they need a little more help and that's when a compass would come in handy. This handmade compass takes seconds to activate, but it works just as well as any computerised equivalent. Give it a try!

TO MAKE A REAL COMPASS, YOU WILL NEED:
- A needle
- A magnet
- A saucer
- A small piece of tissue paper

1. Fill a small saucer with tap water and place it on a flat surface. Now pick the needle up between your forefingers and hold it steady.

2. Carefully use the magnet to stroke the needle from the bottom to its tip at least 50 times. Always stroke the magnet in the same direction, using the same side.

3. Place the needle onto the piece of tissue paper, then gently set the paper afloat on the saucer of water.

4. After a few seconds the tissue paper will soak up the liquid and sink to the bottom of the saucer. Your needle should now be left floating on the surface of the water!

5. Watch as the needle slowly turns to show you a line pointing North/South. The direction of the needlepoint will depend on the direction that you stroked your magnet in.

6. Ask an adult to show you which pole the point of the needle is turning to, then work out NORTH, SOUTH, EAST and WEST. Now you can start navigating!

POKÉ PURPLE!

Even though these amazing Pokémon are displaying their signature purple colouring, everything else is black and white! Pull out your boldest crayons, pencils or felt-tips and then bring the picture to life.

ASH KETCHUM
FRIENDS TO THE END!

THE NEEDS
OF THE THREE!

After their brush with Jupiter, Ash, Brock and Dawn appear to be visited by the same troubling dream. Could the Legendary Pokémon Uxie, Mesprit and Azelf really be using these strange visions to summon the youngsters' help?

Ash, Brock and Dawn smiled as the Lake Trio of Uxie, Mesprit and Azelf appeared before their eyes.

"Finally we get to meet," said Ash.

"So this is what you look like!" cooed Dawn. "Amazing!"

"But I'm kind of wondering why you showed yourselves to all of us?" mused Brock.

At that moment, an oppressive black cloud began to form and swell around the friends.

"Hey! What's wrong?" gasped Ash.

Dawn tried to comfort the Pokémon. "Is there something that you need to say?"

It was not to be. As the mists swirled, the Lake Trio took flight, leaving the pals alone in the darkness.

The friends scrambled in the Pokémon's wake, frantically trying to escape the shadows until…

"What a dream!" Dawn cried, sitting up in bed. She turned to see Ash and Brock also awake on the bunks beside her.

"I just saw the Legendary Pokémon!" she trembled. Brock nodded. "Me too!"

"Did we have the same dream?" stammered Ash, knocked out by the power of the mysterious vision.

Meanwhile at Lake Valor, an ominous dark shape hovered into view. Pokémon Hunter J's ship was casting shadows over the azure water.

"Descend to 500 metres!" ordered the renegade. "Prepare to drop the Galactic bomb!"

Down below, Gary Oak watched the ship with a mixture of awe and dread. He called Professor Rowan to alert him of Hunter J's unwanted presence.

"I'm certain that she's come for the Legendary Pokémon!" replied Rowan, asking Gary to get in touch with his fellow Sinnoh researchers – Yuzo at Lake Verity and Carolina at Lake Acuity.

Gary wasted no time in doing what was asked of him. After calling he summoned Electivire from his Poké Ball to join the Umbreon already at his side.

It was a well-timed decision.

Suddenly a voice behind him called for Toxicroak to use Dark Pulse. Gary wheeled round to see Team Galactic Commander Saturn flanked by two henchmen.

"So you're Team Galactic huh?" shouted Gary. "I'm not going to stand by and let you go! Umbreon, use Psychic."

Umbreon's eyes glowed with energy, but Saturn had Toxicroak respond with X-Scissor. Gary's Umbreon was speedily hurled to the ground.

Gary gasped as Umbreon struggled to its feet, when a noise from above interrupted the battle. The doors beneath Pokémon Hunter J's ship were opening…

UMBREON

The Moonlight Pokémon

When exposed to the light of the moon, Eevee evolves into this Dark-type Pokémon. The yellow rings on Umbreon's body are said to glow in the night.

"Release the Galactic Bomb," ordered Pokémon Hunter J.

Suddenly the monstrous weapon emerged from the hold beneath her ship. It plummeted down and hit the lake, exploding beneath the surface.

There was a blinding flash.

Umbreon and Electivire shielded their eyes while Gary stared open-mouthed at the terrible sight before him. A huge whirlpool had opened up in the centre of the lake and a crackling energy ball was now floating in the sky above the great chasm.

Brock was at his side in seconds.

"I felt it… it's Azelf," winced Ash.

Dawn's eyes grew wide. "You mean like the dream?"

"If that's true," wondered Brock. "Then what was that dream?"

The friends hurriedly contacted Professor Rowan on the videophone. They listened opened-mouthed as the Professor filled them in about Hunter J and Team Galactic's appearances at Lake Valor.

"They've joined forces!" gasped Brock.

"And they're after Azelf," added Dawn.

"The Galactic Bomb," Saturn smirked. "Made out of the meteor taken from Veilstone City – it's powerful enough to open up a hole in space!"

Gary shielded his eyes. "It can't be!"

"You see the Lake Pokémon don't exactly live in a lake," hissed Saturn. "They simply observe our world from another dimension through a portal that looks very much like a lake."

Many miles away, Ash winced in pain and held his head.

Moments later, Professor Rowan began receiving transmissions from Lake Verity and Lake Acuity. Yuzo and Carolina reported that the same things were happening there, too.

"It would appear that the Legendary Pokémon are sending some sort of signal to Ash and his friends," surmised Rowan.

Over at Lake Valor, Gary was doing his best to fight back.

Seeing Hunter J soar overhead on her ferocious Salamence, he called forth Electivire and urged it to use Thunder. But before the Electric-type could do its worst, a bolt from behind sent it reeling once more.

"You stay out of this!" warned Saturn, as his henchmen called a flock of Golbat from their Poké Balls. The Pokémon were sent soaring out across the lake, surrounding the floating ball of energy.

Hunter J ordered Salamence to use Hyper Beam. The move hit the energy ball square on. Gary gasped as the ball evaporated to reveal… Azelf.

Azelf stretched then opened its eyes to find itself surrounded by a flock of Golbat attacking with Supersonic. Luckily however, the Golbat were no match for the Legendary Pokémon. It despatched its attackers easily.

Then, from behind came Hunter J on Salamence. J flicked her wrist blaster, instantly immobilising Azelf. Her victim found itself encased in a bell jar, floating into Saturn's waiting hands.

Miles away Ash, feeling Azelf's suffering, groaned in agony.

From the safety of his headquarters, Cyrus watched the unfolding scenes with delight.

"It has been said for centuries that the Legendary Pokémon were created at the time of the very beginnings of the Universe…" he told his crew. "Those three work in close harmony protecting Sinnoh, but legend also states that if one of them were ever to fall, all three would then have to appear in order to restore balance."

Minutes later, the screens began to hum as reports from the Observation Squads at Lakes Verity and Acuity came in. Both Mesprit and Uxie had appeared and disappeared. It seemed that they had teleported elsewhere.

"We have to do something to help them out!" Ash told Professor Rowan by video link.

"We think the Pokémon are pleading with us to save them all now," said Dawn, still wincing from the pain she'd felt when Mesprit had vanished.

Brock agreed. He'd felt Uxie's pain too.

"We've got to go!" he pressed.

As the threesome prepared to leave, a car pulled up. It was Cynthia, a champion Trainer and friend of Ash and his gang.

"Hop in," she invited.

Back at Lake Valor the legend seemed to be coming true. With Azelf captured, Uxie and Mesprit had no choice but to appear. They too soon found themselves surrounded by Golbat and Hunter J. They let fly with Future Sight, but the bolts seemed to zoom past Hunter J into the ether. In no time at all, Uxie and Mesprit were also trapped in bell jars.

"It's just as Cyrus said it would be!" exclaimed Mars. "If one falls then the rest come tumbling down."

As Cynthia's car motored towards the lakes, Dawn and Brock squirmed in pain.

"They've got Mesprit!" cried Dawn.

Brock nodded. "Uxie too."

"If you want to help them you'll have to take care of Team Galactic first," Cynthia advised. Explaining that their friend Looker was investigating on Mount Coronet, she sped off in that direction.

At Lake Valor, Saturn congratulated Pokémon Hunter J on a job well done.

"You have your payment as agreed," he told her, smiling as she handed over the remaining two Lake Pokémon. Now Team Galactic had the entire Legendary Lake Trio in their clutches!

Hunter J climbed on Salamence, then returned to her ship.

"All right!" ordered the vigilante. "Return to base!"

But before the ship could power away, two bolts of electricity shot from above and blasted the craft, sending it plummeting down into the whirlpool. It exploded in seconds.

"That has to be Mesprit and Uxie's Future Sight," Saturn gasped as he, Mars and Jupiter, watched the plumes of smoke rise from the water. "The power of these Legendary Pokémon is frightening."

On Mount Coronet, Looker was spying on Team Galactic's operations. The task wasn't being made any easier by the chattering presence of his surprise travelling companions – Team Rocket.

"So you're looking for them too," exclaimed James. "What a coincidink!"

The bungling trio offered to help the police officer take out Team Galactic once and for all.

"Slow it down!" hissed Looker. "We need to secure the area first."

Meowth punched the air. "Let's hit 'em, where they hide!"

The trio quickly donned green wigs and uniforms.

"When it comes to disguises we at Team Rocket are like no other," boasted James.

She tailed off as Ash, Dawn and Brock suddenly screamed in pain and clutched their heads.

"It hurts!" cried Ash.

Dawn clutched her ears. "So intense!"

"Much stronger than before," yelped Brock.

At that moment, all three friends disappeared from the car.

"They've been summoned!" exclaimed Cynthia, looking back at her empty seats.

Meanwhile Cynthia was busy filling Ash, Dawn and Brock in on Galactic's plans.

"As of this moment, Galactic has the Lake Trio and the two treasures in its possession," she explained urgently. "Which looks to me like they're fully prepared to call forth Dialga and Palkia."

The Champion paused while the gang took this in.

"Of course Dialga is known as the Ruler of Time and Palkia the Ruler of Space. For two Legendary Pokémon like them to fall under human control is beyond comprehension. Team Galactic might even be able to unleash ancient powers we're not aware of…"

At Galactic's headquarters, Charon and Cyrus had finally unleashed the power of the Red Chain by implanting stones into the heads of Azelf, Uxie and Mesprit. The three, once more in incredible pain, had called their friends to their side.

"The Veilstone Meteor was definitely created from the core substance of the Universe!" Charon gloated. "It's filled with a power that we've now tapped into."

The criminal's face lit up with pleasure as Ash and his pals suddenly appeared in a heap on the floor. "Looks like we've got company!"

"What have you done?" cried Ash, surveying the room.

His shock turned to fury when he spotted the immobilised Lake Pokémon, red stones glinting menacingly in their foreheads.

Jupiter, Saturn and Mars were quick to take position, summoning their Pokémon and spoiling for a fight, until Cyrus stopped them.

"Team Galactic is my creation and you are now in my headquarters," he announced coldly. "We're bringing about a new world order. So we're gathered here to discard the old world of discord and conflict and make a much better one in its place."

"So it was you who stole the Lustrous Orb from the Celestic Ruins!" yelled Ash, seeing the Orbs and the Spear Key displayed on podiums.

"Lose your rage," replied Cyrus calmly. "It only destroys."

"Not when you treat Pokémon that way," countered Dawn. "This has gotta stop. Let them go back to their lake!"

Cyrus simply shook his head.

"That can't be done. They're necessary for us to be able to bring forth the new world."

Brock fizzed with emotion. "That means it's exactly as Cynthia said it was."

"Obviously these children must mean something important if the Legendary Pokémon saw fit to bring them all here," said Cyrus, turning to his team. "We will need to keep them around until our task is completed, just in case."

"You won't get away with it," seethed Ash. "Who cares if you're Team Galactic!"

The irate Trainer called on Pikachu to use Thunderbolt, while Brock and Dawn prepared Croagunk and Piplup for battle.

While a powerful assault begins to take shape against the evil Team Galactic in an attempt to free the three Legendary Pokémon, will our heroes be successful in their mission?
Turn to page 58 to find out!

GOLBAT

ATTACK

Team Galactic's vast swarm of Golbat are on the offensive again! This page is over-run with flocking Pokémon, but can you really get a handle on their attack? Count up each and every Golbat, then write the correct total in the box below.

THERE ARE _____ GOLBAT

POKÉMON FIELD REPORT

Dedicated breeders can be perfectionists when it comes to research! Some might spend hours observing Pokémon in the wild, compiling detailed field reports so they can learn exactly what makes each species tick.

If you could observe any Pokémon in its natural setting, which one would it be? Perhaps mighty Heatran or a quieter breed such as Togekiss or Beautifly? Pick the Pokémon that intrigues you most, then fill this page with an imaginary field report.

DRAW A PICTURE OF YOUR POKÉMON HERE

SPECIES:..................... TYPE:........................

ABILITY:.................... SIZE:...........................

COLOURING:...

DISTINCTIVE MARKINGS:...

....

PREFERRED HABITAT:...

....

UNUSUAL BEHAVIOURS:...............................

....

BEST ATTACK MOVE:..............................

WHY I LIKE THIS POKÉMON:..............

....

....

....

....

NOT MY TYPE!

How confident are you at picking out Pokémon types? This gruelling challenge has been specially selected for a promising young Trainer like you! Study the pictures and then circle the odd one out in each type box.

ELECTRIC
- PICHU
- RAICHU
- LUXRAY
- ALAKAZAM

BUG
- BUDEW
- BURMY
- KRICKETOT
- CASCOON

ICE
- GLALIE
- SNORUNT
- KIRLIA
- GLACEON

FIGHTING
- MACHOP
- RIOLU
- DUSKNOIR
- MACHOKE

DARK

TANGROWTH

ABSOL

SNEASEL

UMBREON

NORMAL

CHANSEY

AIPOM

CLEFABLE

MAGBY

WATER

GOLDUCK

MAGIKARP

MUNCHLAX

PIPLUP

DUAL-TYPE

GIRAFARIG

TENTACRUEL

HERACROSS

RAPIDASH

TYPE TIME

Did you know that there are 17 types that are use to categorise Pokémon and their moves? Fill in the missing letters to complete this inventory then keep it to hand for future battles.

1. F _ R _

2. WA _ ER

3. GRA _ _

4. ELEC _ _ IC

5. _ ORM _ _

6. _ CE

7. _ IGHTING

8. P _ _ SON

9. _ ROUND

10. FL _ _ NG

11. PSYCH _ _

2. B _ G

13. _ OCK

14. G _ _ ST

15. DR _ _ ON

16. DA _ _

17. _ TE _ L

51

UMBREON, ELECTIVIRE -
COME ON OUT!

POKÉMON
POWER

Weavile, Lucario and Gallade are three of the fiercest Pokémon in the Sinnoh region. Each species makes a tough battle opponent – known for its fighting ability and skill. Use your brightest shades to colour in these mighty titans.

When you've finished sign your name at the bottom of the frame.

Sign your name here:

FOLLOW THE LADDERS!

1

Hides thorny whips in its arms

Grass- and Poison-type

Known as the Bouquet Pokémon

2

Extremely cautious

Long super-fluffy ears

Normal-type

3

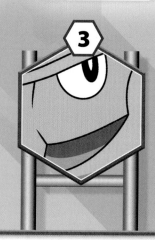

Has a hard shell

Turtwig's next Evolution

Prefers to live near water

Climb down each of these ladders – what do you think you'll find?
Study the clues on each rung, then stick in a picture of the Pokémon that
owns each one. Do you have the skill to guess the identity of all six species?

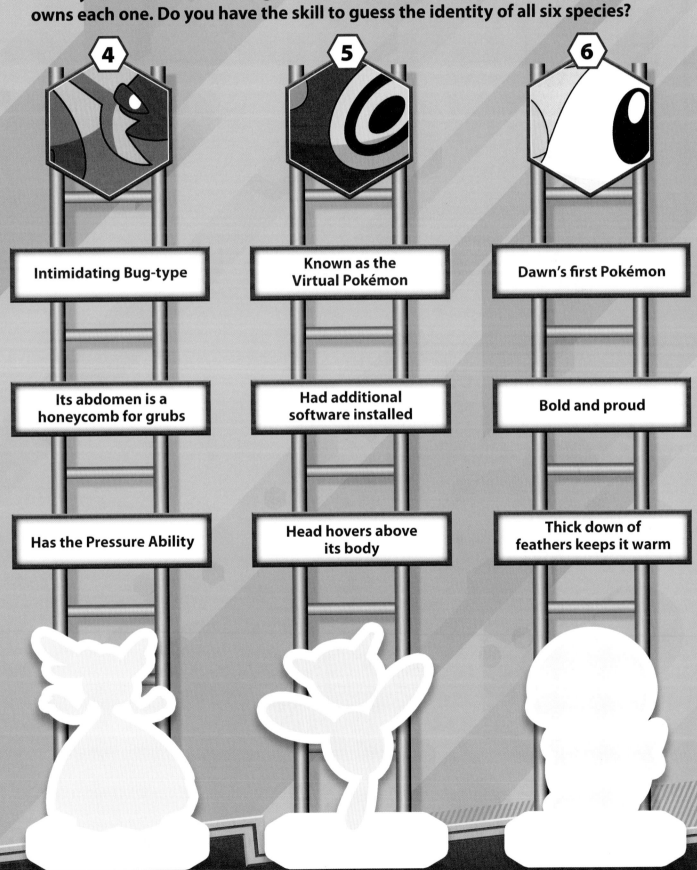

4

Intimidating Bug-type

Its abdomen is a honeycomb for grubs

Has the Pressure Ability

5

Known as the Virtual Pokémon

Had additional software installed

Head hovers above its body

6

Dawn's first Pokémon

Bold and proud

Thick down of feathers keeps it warm

MIRROR MIRROR

This Legendary Pokémon has two awe-inspiring forms. In this guise it is said to dwell in the mysterious Reverse World, a parallel dimension that mirrors the regular world. Can you find some bold crayons or pens and bring this impressive Pokémon to life?

GIRATINA (ALTERED FORME)

What is the name of this Legendary Ghost- and Dragon-type? Hold this page up a mirror and its identity will be revealed. Write the name in here.

_ _ _ _ _ _ _ _ (_ _ _ _ _ _ _ _)

DOUBLE BLUFF!

Do you know the name of this Johto Pokémon? It's an amphibious species that seems to be oblivious to pain. It is also known as the Water Fish Pokémon.

The correct name is hidden in this letter grid. Help Ash reveal it by crossing out all the letters that feature more than once. Now reorder the remaining ones and write the Pokémon into the box at the bottom of the page.

E	C	K	S	P	V	C	C	Y	Z
X	M	X	V	M	D	X	V	L	R
N	B	K	D	J	P	W	U	T	Y
F	Q	J	Y	Z	K	O	F	W	D
F	T	P	F	A	M	H	T	L	B
C	X	K	Y	X	Y	Z	Z	H	T
V	D	J	V	B	D	K	G	X	F
N	F	C	F	N	Z	J	M	Y	O
J	I	N	T	D	D	T	R	L	N
W	Z	J	L	W	L	J	C	W	B

The Pokémon is _ _ _ _ _ _ _ _

Got it right? Well done! Stick a picture of Ash and Pikachu celebrating in here.

THE BATTLE FINALE OF LEGEND!

With the odds stacked against them, our heroes are attempting to thwart the evil plans of Team Galactic. Can the friends do what's necessary to free the Legendary Lake Trio and ensure the future of the Universe itself?

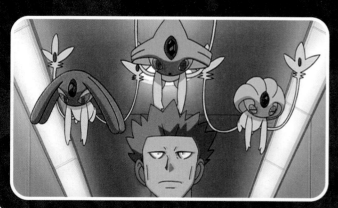

In Team Galactic's hidden mountain lair, Ash, Brock and Dawn were attempting to rescue Azelf, Mesprit and Uxie.

The plucky pals had already used Piplup's BubbleBeam and Pikachu's Thunderbolt to fend off attacks from Mars and Jupiter's Purugly and Skuntank.

Ash cheered as their Pokémon smashed the jars containing the immobilised Lake Trio. The Legendary Pokémon were free, but before they could reach them, Saturn ordered his Toxicroak to use Sludge Bomb.

Pikachu, Piplup and Croagunk were sent tumbling through the air, stunned.

After checking their Pokémon were OK, Ash and his friends expected the Lake Trio to be making their way towards them, but instead Azelf, Mesprit and Uxie just hung in the air. Red stones like the one Looker had found at the Ironworks glinted on each of their foreheads. They seemed hypnotised.

"Azelf, what's wrong?" cried Ash, checking its vacant expression.

"Mesprit," asked Dawn. "Don't you recognise us?" Galactic leader Cyrus strode up behind the three floating Pokémon.

"We have the Red Chain which now possesses the Powers of the Original One," he announced arrogantly. "They are under my complete control."

"According to legend these powers are responsible for reshaping our entire world! No Pokémon is able to withstand them!" Charon cackled.

It was finally time for Cyrus to reveal the full horror of his heinous ambition.

"It is with these original powers that I will create a new world order!" he cried.

"What's going to happen to us now?" Dawn whispered as she, Ash and Brock were rounded up and thrown into a cell within the Galactic helicopter.

"Cyrus is using us as hostages so Uxie and the others will do what he tells them," Brock explained.

"We're part of his back-up plan – in case they break free from his control."

"We've got to get out of here!" decided Ash. "Those Pokémon came to see us in our dreams!"

Brock and Dawn agreed.

"We can't let them down!" added the Coordinator.

Meanwhile deep in the mountains, Team Rocket and Looker were intent on their own mission. Disguised in Team Galactic uniforms they'd overthrown the guards barring the entrance to the Spear Pillar.

The spies hid as Team Galactic's helicopter loomed into view. It landed and Jupiter, Mars and Saturn emerged, followed by Cyrus himself.

"He's da Team Galactic big cheese?" asked Meowth. No one had time to answer. Jupiter immediately had her Skuntank direct a fearsome Flamethrower move on the intruders. The Commander hadn't been fooled by their bogus costumes for a second!

"My own mother wouldn't have known me in this disguise," moaned James as Team Rocket and Looker were herded into the helicopter.

Within minutes the despondent spies found themselves imprisoned with Ash, Brock and Dawn.

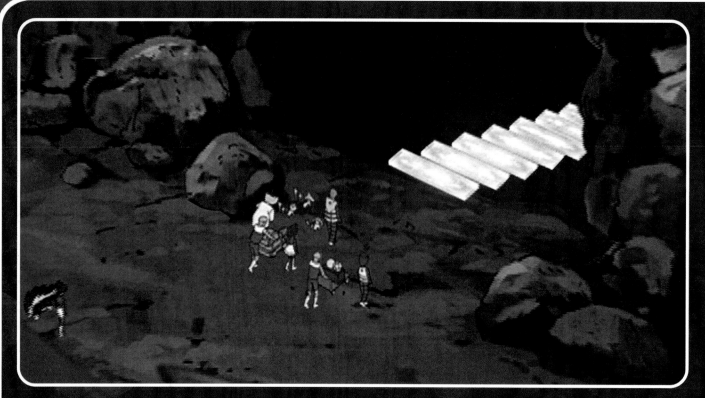

With their enemies safely behind bars, Team Galactic walked to the entrance of Spear Pillar.

Saturn lifted the Spear Key out of a briefcase and held it up towards the metal gates. The gates vanished as if by magic, revealing steps leading down into blackness.

"Exactly as it was written in ancient times," smiled Cyrus, as he made his way down the steps flanked by Mars, Saturn and Charon.

"Awwww…!" moaned Jupiter, as her cohorts disappeared. "Why do I have to stay behind and guard this thing anyway?"

Jupiter was so busy complaining to her Skuntank, she didn't hear trouble approaching.

Cynthia's Garchomp swooped down, taking out Skuntank and overpowering its owner.

Right on cue, Cynthia screeched up in her car. "Now, where are they?" she demanded. Jupiter had no choice but to lead Cynthia into the helicopter to find her friends.

Ash, Brock and Dawn beamed with delight as she freed them, while Team Rocket and Looker were happy to stay behind and guard Jupiter and the remaining Galactic crew.

"There's nothing like a little payback time to soothe the savage ego," Jessie taunted as James tied Jupiter and three other Galactic guards together.

Deep underground, Cyrus and his team had at last found the Spear Pillar.

"In perfect shape after all these years," Charon sighed, gazing at the triangular stone pattern surrounded by pillars upon which Cyrus placed the two Orbs and the three Lake Pokémon.

"Azelf, Mesprit and Uxie, hear me now!" called Cyrus. "Transfer your ancient powers to the Adamant and Lustrous Orbs. Using the infinite Original Powers, connect time and space!"

As energy levels rose around Mount Coronet, the skies above darkened as thick black clouds swirled ominously together.

Beneath the mountain Cyrus raised his arms dramatically.

"Dialga and Palkia, the time has come," he bellowed. "Reveal yourselves!"

The air crackled expectantly. Charon fired a portable cannon and two red chains shot out. Suddenly the outlines of Dialga and Palkia became visible! The chains encircled the awesome Pokémon, binding them tight.

Just then, a blast ripped through the air and destroyed the cannon, sending the Team Galactic henchmen flying. Pikachu, Piplup and Croagunk swooped down from above on Staraptor, Garchomp and Gliscor.

Saturn called out for his Toxicroak, but this time Croagunk was ready. When the Poison- and Fighting-type pair met mid-air, Croagunk sent its rival flying with a single punch.

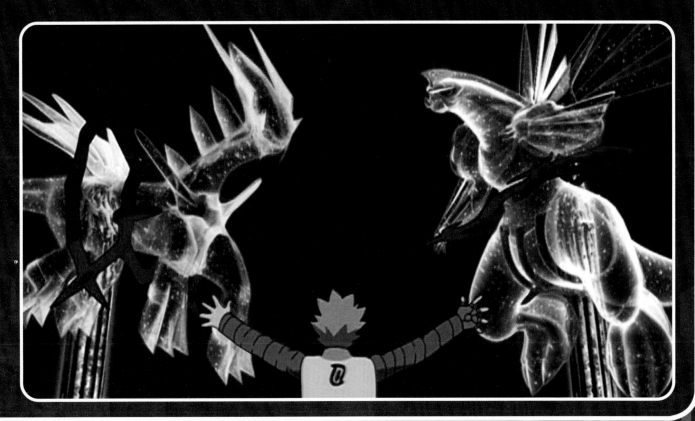

Ash, Dawn and Brock arrived just in time to see Brock's loyal Pokémon land safely.

"Awesome Croagunk, good job!" called the breeder.

The friends paused to take in the terrible scene before them.

"Dialga, Palkia and the three Legendary Lake Guardians!" gasped Cynthia. "I've always wanted to meet them, but certainly not like this."

Energy levels dimmed and the shapes of Dialga and Palkia began to disappear.

Ash had Staraptor and Gliscor return to their Poké Balls, as he and his friends ran to comfort the Lake Trio.

"Azelf, it's me!" said Ash. "Are you OK?"
"I've got you, Mesprit," added Dawn, gently cradling the Legendary Pokémon in her arms.

"I'm coming Uxie!" reassured Brock.

"Stop it Cyrus!" yelled Ash, but Team Galactic were far from ready to quit.

Mars called out Purugly. The Team Galactic guards also called forth their Golbat. But Ash and Dawn called again on Pikachu and Piplup's impressive moves. Despite their tiny size, the duo quickly floored Team Galactic's Pokémon.

"Here's our chance to save the Lake Guardians!" yelled Cynthia.

While Team Galactic regrouped for attack, the friends sent their Pokémon soaring towards the Lake Trio, blasting the scarlet stones away from their heads.

Cynthia turned victoriously to face Cyrus.

"You no longer have the power to control Dialga or Palkia!" she shouted.

"I wouldn't be so sure!" came the troubling reply. Cyrus lifted his palm to reveal a last gleaming stone from the red chain glinting there. There was a rush of energy and Dialga and Palkia returned, except this time they appeared in their true forms.

"No!" cried Ash as the massive Pokémon struggled in their bonds, roaring and screeching in pain.

"They can't resist!" smirked Saturn. "It's impossible to break free from the Red Chain containing the Original Powers."

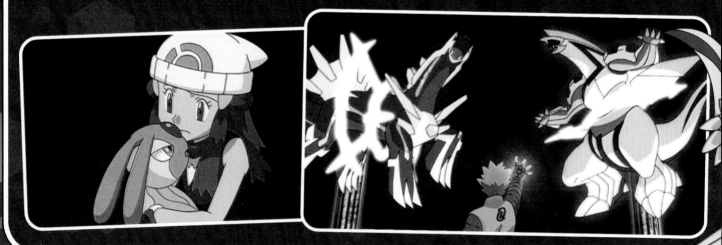

All seemed lost, but suddenly the Lake Trio began to glow. Brock, Dawn and Ash immediately felt warm.

"What's going on?" Ash asked.

"They must be willing this to happen," Brock answered, somehow hearing Uxie's thoughts.

All three friends understood that the Lake Trio were asking them to help save Dialga and Palkia.

Their hearts had truly become one with the Legendary Pokémon!

Cyrus seemed unaware of this special bond. He held his arms aloft, commanding Dialga and Palkia to release their powers and create a new universe.

"It's time!" declared Jupiter. "A new world is being born… and the old one destroyed!"

"Get away!" cried Cynthia as streams of light and energy flowed from the Pokémon's mouths.

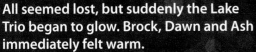

The energy beams clashed above the centre of the stone triangle, forming an ever-expanding hole, which opened to reveal distant stars and planets.

"Our new world!" boomed Cyrus.

Energy levels soared dangerously and on the surface the instruments at Professor Rowan's complex ticked dangerously upwards. It looked as if all Sinnoh was about to be destroyed.

63

But it wasn't in Ash Ketchum's nature to give up, especially when the world's very existence depended on it!

"I won't let you…." he yelled, calling for Pikachu to aim its Thunderbolt at the red chains.

Following his lead, Dawn had Piplup use BubbleBeam while Brock's Croagunk aimed Poison Sting. With one, last, massive effort Cynthia turned Garchomp's formidable Draco Meteor on the chains too.

"If we can release Dialga and Palkia from them," she cried. "We might be able to stop the creation of the new world!"

But Cyrus harnessed the power of both Dialga and Palkia, turning their Roar of Time and Spatial Rend moves on the gang.

Just when it looked as though Team Galactic had proved themselves to be unstoppable, Uxie, Mesprit and Azelf stepped in. They used their special powers to dispel the force of the blows.

"You did that for us?" marvelled Ash.

"Thanks you three!" said Brock.

But Cyrus's new universe still continued to grow. Mars and Saturn suggested all Team Galactic members pass through immediately, but their leader had other ideas.

"I have no need for you," he yelled cruelly. "This new world belongs to me alone. You could never understand what it truly means!"

While his followers reeled, Cynthia spotted an opportunity.

"Let's attack those rings once more!" she urged. This time the Lake Pokémon also turned their powers on the chain. With an almighty crack, the chains vanished and Dialga and Palkia slumped to the ground. With their freedom, the alternative universe began to shrink away.

"I guess this is the end…" sighed Charon, but Cyrus could not give up on his dream.

Before the portal could close he stepped through into his new universe, disappearing forever.

"Do you think everything will be back to normal now?" Dawn asked hopefully.

To her terror however, energy levels continued to rise.

Dialga and Palkia writhed with fury, blasting energy from their mouths. Would Sinnoh soon cease to exist?

Brock, Ash and Dawn sheltered behind a pillar with their Pokémon and the Lake Trio, but Cynthia warned them that if they didn't do something soon, the region would be destroyed.

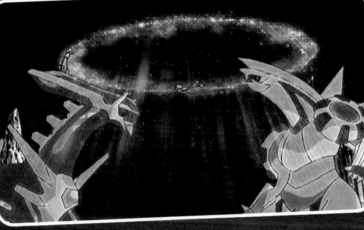

Suddenly, the Lake Pokémon began to communicate again with their friends.

"Combine our hearts as one," Dawn translated. "And please save Dialga and Palkia!"

"OK Azelf, do it!" commanded Ash and he, Dawn and Brock sent the Lake Pokémon upwards to calm the tormented pair.

Flying in circles, the Lake Trio created a twinkling opening, sending Dialga and Palkia back through to their realm. Peace returned to Sinnoh once more.

Ash, Dawn and Brock were ecstatic, but Team Rocket seemed just as thrilled.

"We beat Team Galactic at their own game!" crowed James.

"Sure did, and now this old world is all ours!" said Jessie.

Meowth grinned as their hot air balloon took off again. "An' once 'da Boss gets wind a' 'dis we'll get a windfall!"

"Thank you!" beamed Cynthia, turning to Ash, Brock and Dawn. "Sinnoh is still here because you protected it."

"If that's true then it's because we had Piplup, Mesprit and everyone else helping out," giggled Dawn. "Isn't that right, Piplup?"

And so, as Team Galactic's evil ambitions are finally put to an end, no doubt our heroes will continue to pursue their hopes and dreams, as their journey continues!

THE END

"So Azelf, Uxie and Mesprit," smiled Ash, a little later. "Why in the world did you go and choose us?"

Cynthia explained to the friends that the Lake Trio had obviously sensed how much they cared about Pokémon.

MESPRIT

ANSWERS

Pages 6-7
Sinnoh Sum-up
Map happy
1. True.
2. False (Forest).
3. True.
4. False. It is a wetland area that is always boggy and flood-soaked.
5. False. It is a port city.
6. True.
7. False. It has several.
8. False. It has eight.

Pages 8-9
Enter Ash And Pikachu!
Ash
Ash Ketchum is a determined young **Trainer** who's come a long way since he first left his home in **Pallet** Town! Through determination, skill and hard work he's managed to earn himself a batch of **Gym badges** that would make any Pokémon Master proud! Some, like Ash's rival, **Paul**, might say that the youngster is hasty and hot-headed, but his refusal to give up has awarded him the edge in many **Pokémon** battles!

Pikachu
Type: **Electric**
Ability: Static
Height: 0.4m
Weight: 6.0kg
This Pokémon dwells in forests and woodlands, living in large, social groups. It uses its large cheek pouches to store **electricity**. Pikachu is evolved from **Pichu**.

1. STARAPTOR / 2. GROTLE / 3. BUIZEL / 4. GIBLE / 5. MONFERNO

Pages 12-13
Definitely Dawn!
1. MAMOSWINE / 2. BUNEARY / 3. PIPLUP / 4. PACHIRISU

Dawn's new Pokémon is **CYNDAQUIL!**

Pages 14-15
Team Rocket Time
1. He can communicate using human speech.
2. A very wealthy one. James' parents were millionaires.
3. Giovanni
4. Hot air balloon
5. Twerps

Poké Pals
WOBBUFFET
SEVIPER
YANMEGA
MIME JR.
CARNIVINE

Page 16
Land Of Legends
Poké Facts:
1. Dialga and Palkia live in other dimensions.
2. Palkia has the Pressure Ability.
3. Fiction!
4. Since ancient times, both Pokémon have featured in Sinnoh legends.
5. Fiction!
6. Statues of them are sometimes found near ancient ruins.
7. Fiction!
8. Dialga has no Evolutions.
9. Fiction!

Page 18
Ways Through The Waves

Page 19
Choose Your Cherrim!
G is an exact match.

Pages 20-21
All Of A Dozen?

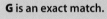

Pages 30-31
Team Rocket Challenges YOU!
1. c. Blissey
2. b. It has a floatation sac that inflates like a collar.
3. b. Chatot
4. a. Grass-type
5. a. Jolteon
6. c. The EleSquirrel Pokémon
7. a. Azumarill
8. b. It sprays toxic fumes from its tail
9. a. Shellos
10. b. Dustox

Team Rocket Challenges YOU!
(continued)
11. b. Aipom
12. b. Twice its height
13. a. Magmortar
14. b. A crack in a keystone
15. c. Meditite

Page 34
Rule It Out!
MURKROW

Page 35
Habitat Match
1. B / 2. F / 3. A / 4. E / 5. D / 6. C

Page 36
New Moves
SWIFT / FLAME WHEEL / SMOKESCREEN

Page 48
Golbat Attack!
There are **21** Golbat.

Pages 50-51
Not My Type!
ELECTRIC - ALAKAZAM
BUG - BUDEW
ICE - KIRLIA
FIGHTING - DUSKNOIR
DARK - TANGROWTH
NORMAL - MAGBY
WATER - MUNCHLAX
DUAL-TYPE - RAPIDASH

Type-time
1. FIRE / 2. WATER / 3. GRASS /
4. ELECTRIC / 5. NORMAL / 6. ICE /
7. FIGHTING / 8. POISON / 9. GROUND /
10. FLYING / 11. PSYCHIC / 12. BUG /
13. ROCK / 14. GHOST / 15. DRAGON /
16. DARK / 17. STEEL

Pages 54-55
Follow The Ladders!
1. ROSERADE / 2. LOPUNNY /
3. GROTLE / 4. VESPIQUEN /
5. PORYGON-Z / 6. PIPLUP

Page 56
Mirror Mirror
GIRATINA (ALTERED FORME)

Page 57
Double Bluff!

The Pokémon is QUAGSIRE!

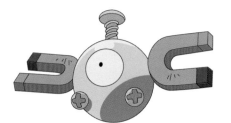

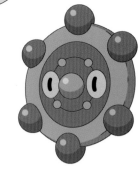

VESPIQUEN

PIPLUP

LOPUNNY

PDR4GDN-Z   GRDTLE   RDSERADE